SPOOKY SITES

EMILY'S BRIDGE

THOMAS KINGSLEY TROUPE

A Shark Book
SEAHORSE PUBLISHING

Teaching Tips for Caregivers:

You can help your child learn by encouraging them to read widely, both as a leisure activity and as a way of satisfying their curiosity about the world. Reading helps build a strong foundation in language and literacy skills that will help your child succeed in school. This high-interest book will appeal to all readers in intermediate and middle school grades.

Use the following suggestions to help your child grow as a reader.

- Encourage them to read independently at home.
- Encourage them to practice reading aloud.
- Encourage activities that require reading.
- Establish a regular reading time.
- Have your child ask and answer questions about what they read.

Teaching Tips for Teachers:

Engage students throughout the reading process by asking questions like these.

Before Reading
- Ask, "What do you already know about this topic?"
- Ask, "What do you want to learn about this topic?"

During Reading
- Ask, "What is the author trying to teach you?"
- Ask, "How is this like something you have read or seen before?"
- Ask, "How do the text features (headings, index, etc.) help you understand the topic?"

After Reading
- Ask, "What interesting or fun fact did you learn?"
- Ask, "What questions do you still have about the topic? How could you find the answers?"

TABLE OF CONTENTS

An Ordinary Old Bridge? 4
Who Was Emily? 6
Chills and Scratches 10
Voices and Music 12
Apparitions 14
Real or Hoax? 17
Proof in the Graveyard? 18
Be a Paranormal Investigator! 20
Glossary 22
Index 23
After Reading Questions 23
About the Author 24

An Ordinary Old Bridge?

It's a dark and quiet night in New England. The moon is trapped behind thick clouds, casting a faint glow. The headlight on your bike reveals a covered bridge ahead. It's wooden and old, with a pointy roof. You can hear a brook bubbling below.

As you ride slowly across the old bridge, you feel a chill. A voice whispers lightly in your ear. The wood creaks...or is that the sound of a rope? Your heart races, and you pedal faster. Something doesn't want you there. Time to go!

Who Was Emily?

Gold Brook Covered Bridge is an old, wooden, covered bridge in Stowe, Vermont. It was built in 1844 as a way for travelers to cross Gold Brook. The bridge is a little over 50 feet (15 meters) long. It looks like any of the other beautiful covered bridges in Vermont.

Except…this bridge has long been known as Emily's Bridge. Why?

FRIGHTENING FACTS

Vermont has more covered bridges than any other state in America. There are about 104 of them. Thankfully, only one of them might be haunted!

Legend has it that in the mid-1800s, a young woman named Emily planned to meet her boyfriend here. They hoped to run away together and get married. When her boyfriend didn't show up, Emily was filled with despair.

Emily was heartbroken and **jilted**. Some believe she decided to take her own life. It is said she hanged herself from the wooden rafters above the bridge. Inside the bridge, her spirit is now stuck for eternity, waiting for her lover.

There is also another version of the tale. Some believe that Emily waited at a church for her sweetheart. When he left her standing at the altar, she rode her horse-drawn carriage to confront him. After losing control, she crashed into the brook, killing herself and all the horses. Her ghost now haunts the area, scaring anyone who crosses the bridge.

Chills and Scratches

As the tale of Emily's **tragedy** spread, people became curious. Travelers reported feeling a chill whenever they crossed the bridge. Many believed it came from sensing Emily's ghost who was still angry that her boyfriend left her waiting.

Other visitors to the bridge claimed they were scratched by something unseen. People walking through the covered bridge could feel something sharp scrape their skin.

Cars driving over the bridge weren't always safe either. Drivers claimed to hear scraping noises on the roofs of their vehicles. Were Emily's feet dragging across the cars as they passed beneath the spot where she hanged?

SCRAPE!

Voices and Music

As if chills and scratches from Emily's ghost weren't scary enough, some people have heard whispers and talking near the bridge. The voice is sometimes hard to understand, and it doesn't seem to come from any definite direction. People say that when the voice is clearer, it sounds like a woman screaming and pleading for help.

FRIGHTENING FACTS

Paranormal investigators try to capture EVP, or Electronic Voice Phenomena. They use audio recorders to record EVP, hoping to hear voices from ghosts and spirits.

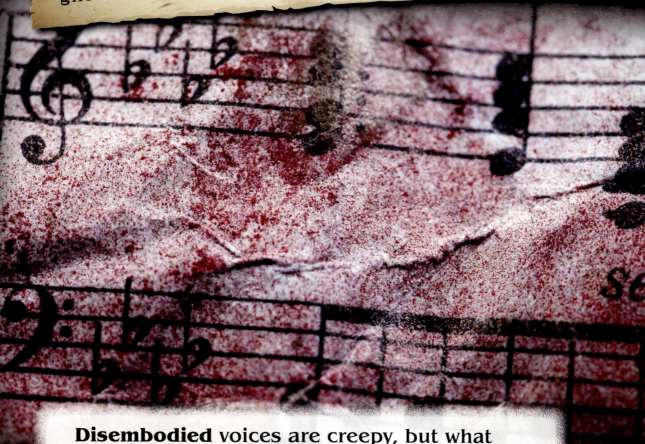

Disembodied voices are creepy, but what about ghostly music? A few bridge visitors have reported hearing unearthly music in the wind. The low, slow tune sounded like it was being played by a harp. It seemed to be coming from inside the bridge. But when investigated, there were no instruments to be found.

Apparitions

There have been reports of **apparitions** appearing on the bridge at night. People have claimed to see a white figure lingering nearby, watching them. Curious investigators have taken photos that show a white mist.

A group of young people in a car said they saw an **entity** of a woman approach their parked vehicle. It jiggled the door handles, trying to get inside. When the doors wouldn't open, the ghost **dissipated** until there was nothing there.

FRIGHTENING FACTS

It is hard to determine if photos show paranormal activity or not. Photos can be edited and altered to make them look much creepier than they really are. Sadly, not everyone is honest with their evidence!

Real or Hoax?

Does Emily really haunt the old bridge? Some believe it's not real and just a **hoax**. A woman named Nancy Stead claims that she made up the story years ago. She lived near the bridge in the 1970s.

Nancy was tired of disrespectful people having loud parties at the nearby swimming hole. She says she created the ghost story to scare people away from the once-peaceful area.

Over time, news of Emily's tragic tale spread. Interest in the bridge grew. If Nancy is right about inventing the story, her plan backfired. More people than ever flock to the bridge to witness the **paranormal** events for themselves.

Proof in the Graveyard?

Researchers have looked into the town's history to see if "Emily" actually existed. They were not able to find any records of her birth or her accidental death. There are a few graves in the nearby Old Yard Cemetery bearing the name Emily. The date of death on one of them seems to line up. Could it be her?

Emily's Bridge is still standing in Stowe, Vermont. Thrill-seekers and paranormal investigators visit the bridge in large numbers. The legend has turned the area into a bit of a tourist destination. Some of the stores in town sell Emily's Bridge souvenirs!

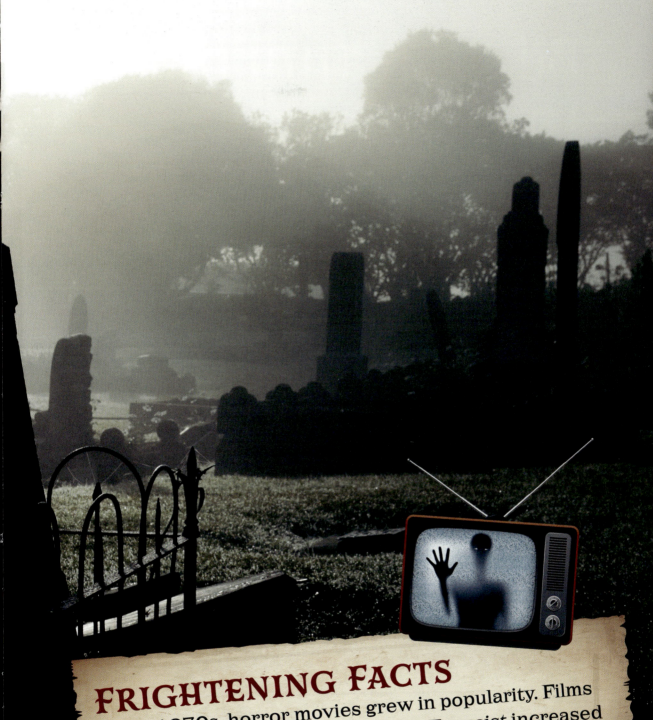

FRIGHTENING FACTS

In the 1970s, horror movies grew in popularity. Films like The Amityville Horror and The Exorcist increased interest in scary places like Emily's Bridge.

Be a Paranormal Investigator!

Whether it's really haunted or not, Emily's Bridge is still a creepy place for the curious to explore. Did someone named Emily really die there? Is her spirit truly stuck there for eternity? No one knows for sure. The **lore** is fascinating regardless!

Do you want to be a paranormal investigator? You can! All you really need is a flashlight, an audio recorder, and some bravery. Go to a dark, creepy place. Look around and ask questions. Record the whole EVP session. When you play the recording back, you might hear strange things. Is it something paranormal trying to talk to you? It could be!

Glossary

apparitions (ap-puh-RI-shuhnz): supernatural appearances of people or things; ghosts or specters

disembodied (dis-uhm-BAH-deed): disconnected from a solid form or a body

dissipated (DIS-uh-pay-tid): broke up, scattered, or vanished

entity (EN-tuh-tee): something that exists; a being

hoax (hohks): a trick that makes people believe something that is not true

jilted (JIL-tid): cast aside by a loved one without care

legend (LEG-uhnd): a story handed down from earlier times; a story that may be based on fact, but that may not be entirely true

lore (lor): spoken knowledge or tradition passed down through cultures

paranormal (pair-uh-NOR-muhl): something that cannot be explained by science

tragedy (TRAJ-i-dee): an event that ends in disaster and sadness

Index

boyfriend 7, 10

covered bridge 4, 6, 10

eternity 8, 20

evidence 15

EVP 13, 21

ghost(s) 9, 10, 12–14, 17

Gold Brook 6

investigator(s) 13, 14, 18, 21

Old Yard Cemetery 18

Stead, Nancy 17

Stowe, Vermont 6, 18

After Reading Questions

1. What legend explains Emily's Bridge?

2. Describe three ways in which people say Emily's ghost makes its presence known on the bridge.

3. Why is it hard to verify evidence of paranormal activity?

4. What qualities of a covered bridge make it a good site for a ghost story?

About the Author

Thomas Kingsley Troupe is the author of over 200 books for young readers. When he's not writing, he enjoys reading, playing video games, and investigating haunted places with the Twin Cities Paranormal Society. Otherwise, he's probably taking a nap or something. Thomas lives in Woodbury, Minnesota, with his two sons.

Written by: Thomas Kingsley Troupe
Design by: Under the Oaks Media
Editor: Kim Thompson

Photo credits: Brain Jannsen/Alamy: p. 16; All other images by Shutterstock

Library of Congress PCN Data
Emily's Bridge / Thomas Kingsley Troupe
Spooky Sites
ISBN 979-8-8904-2690-1 (hard cover)
ISBN 979-8-8904-2718-2 (paperback)
ISBN 979-8-8904-2746-5 (EPUB)
ISBN 979-8-8904-2774-8 (eBook)
Library of Congress Control Number: 2023922885

Printed in the United States of America.

Seahorse Publishing Company
seahorsepub.com

Copyright © 2025 **SEAHORSE PUBLISHING COMPANY**

All rights reserved. No part of this publication may be reproduced, stored in a retrieval system or be transmitted in any form or by any means, electronic, mechanical, photocopying, recording, or otherwise, without the prior written permission of Seahorse Publishing Company.

Published in the United States
Seahorse Publishing
PO Box 771325
Coral Springs, FL 33077